Agile Engineering and Testing Practices for a Development Team
Preparing for the PSD I Exam

Part of the Agile Education Series™

2

Agile Ice Breaker

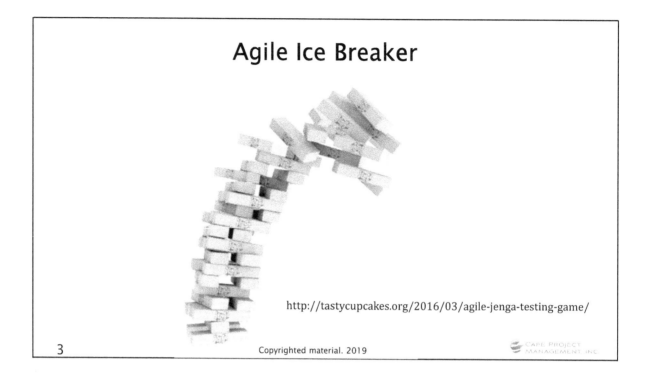

http://tastycupcakes.org/2016/03/agile-jenga-testing-game/

3

Continuing Education

□ This course provides education credits for the following certifications:

  ◘ Continuing Certification for PMPs & PMI-ACPs: 7 PDUs Category: Technical

  ◘ PMI-ACP Application: 7 Agile Education Contact Hours

  ◘ Scrum Alliance SEUs for CSP Application and Maintenance: 7 SEUs Category C: Outside Events

4

Course Objectives

- Define Agile Engineering Best Practices
- Understand Quality Practices in Agile
- Prepare for the PSD I or CAPe-Dev certification
- Have fun!

Agenda

1. Agile Lifecycle Management
2. Agile Engineering Overview
3. Agile Test Strategies
4. Lifecycle Testing
5. Non-Functional Testing
6. Test Automation
7. Measurement & Metrics
8. Implementation

Agile Practices for a Development Team

Announcements

- Participant materials
  - Slides
  - Exercises
- Breaks

7   Copyrighted material. 2019

Agile Lifecycle Management Overview

Module 1

Copyrighted material. 2019

What is Application Lifecycle Management (ALM)?

plan

code

release

Application
Lifecycle
Management

build

test

- Involves managing the application lifecycle through governance, development and operations.
- ALM always begins with an idea, which leads to the development of the application.
- After the application is created, the next step is deployment in a live environment.
- Once the application loses its business value, it reaches the end of life, where it is no longer used.

9

CAPE PROJECT
MANAGEMENT INC

An Effective ALM Approach Involves:

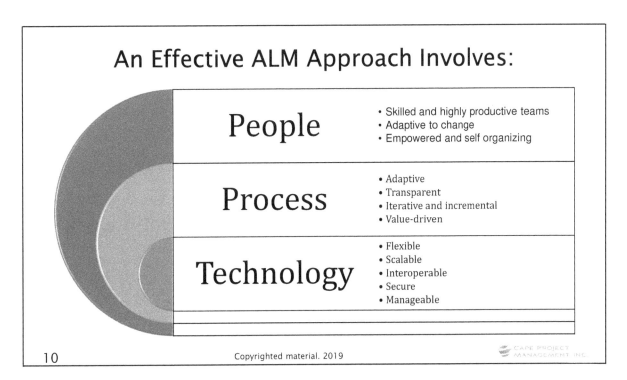

People	• Skilled and highly productive teams • Adaptive to change • Empowered and self organizing
Process	• Adaptive • Transparent • Iterative and incremental • Value-driven
Technology	• Flexible • Scalable • Interoperable • Secure • Manageable

10

CAPE PROJECT
MANAGEMENT INC

Typical ALM Challenges

"We don't have good visibility into project status"

"Our teams are not communicating effectively"

"Requirements are not sufficiently defined or tracked"

"We need lightweight, agile development processes"

"Software is not adequately tested"

"Cost of maintaining and operating the solution exceeds the business benefit"

11   Copyrighted material. 2019

Goals of ALM

- ☐ Teams reduce rework
- ☐ Improve development processes
- ☐ Attain higher-quality of products
- ☐ Achieve timely completion of projects
- ☐ Ensure end-to-end monitoring between work items
- ☐ Reduce cost
- ☐ Recognize lifecycle is broader than SDLC

12   Copyrighted material. 2019

ALM Practice Areas

- Architecture and Design
- User Experience
- Requirements Management
- Software Coding Quality
- Software Configuration Management

- Data Management
- Project Management
- Deployment and Operations
- Quality Assurance and Test
- Application Delivery

Copyrighted material. 2019

Architecture and Design: Challenges

- Functionality is repeated in several different applications
- There is very little or no overall architecture and architectural standards
- A minor change can cause massive headaches:
  - Time consuming to implement
  - Costly
  - A change in one area breaks functionality in another area
- There is very little direction for the future of the application

Copyrighted material. 2019

User Experience: Challenges

- Poor UX in internal facing applications cost money
  - Productivity is negatively impacted
    - Switching between screens to complete a single task
    - Copy and paste between screens
  - Data capture errors impact on the quality of data
- External facing web sites with a poor user experience will lose your company business

15   Copyrighted material. 2019

Requirements Management: Challenges

- Poor requirements are expensive
  - Development time is lengthened
  - Developers spend time clarifying requirements rather than developing software
  - Requirements are incorrectly implemented leading to project failure
  - Redevelopment has to occur which increases the cost of the application overall
- Frustrated and unhappy developers

16   Copyrighted material. 2019

Software Coding Quality: Challenges

- Poor code quality is expensive
  - Higher defect rate
  - Expensive to make changes
    - Difficult to find the right place
    - Learning curve for new developers
  - Security weaknesses
  - Performance issues
- Frustrated and unhappy developers

Software Configuration Management: Challenges

- Poor software configuration management is expensive
  - Reintroduction of previously fixed bugs
  - Lost source code
  - Confusion as to which is the current version
  - Development has to halt when a Production bug has to be fixed
  - The incorrect version of the application is released into the Production environment

Data Management: Challenges

- Lost data – poor back-up procedures
- Unable to roll back to previous version of the database
- Poor application performance due to poor DB design
- "Unmaintainable" stored procedures
- Data structures become convoluted
- Column names no longer describes the data it represent

19

Project Management: Challenges

- Process is not adaptive
- Projects are late
- Projects run over budget
- 90% syndrome
- Overworked developers
- Overtime, stress
- Us vs. Them syndrome

20

Deployment and Operations: Challenges

- Wrong versions are deployed
- Deployment takes too long
- Bugs aren't fixed quickly enough
- Source of a bug is not identified soon enough
- Bugs are not reported to the correct team
  - Is it a network issue?
  - Not enough capacity on a server?
  - A software configuration error?
  - A real bug in the code?

21   Copyrighted material. 2019

Quality Assurance and Test: Challenges

- Testing doesn't start with requirements
- Requirements might be misunderstood and therefore incorrectly programmed
- Not all areas are tested
  - Poor performance in Production – Stress and Performance testing
  - Users will only test the paths they expect to use – edge cases might not be tested
  - Some functionality gets tested over and over while other bits and pieces don't get tested at all
  - Poor impression is created and Business loses confidence in the application

22   Copyrighted material. 2019

Application Delivery: Challenges

- ☐ If your application delivery methodology is too cumbersome you will lag too far behind the customer
- ☐ This will cause the business to lose the competitive edge
- ☐ Big bang approaches
    - ☐ Requirements are out of date even before you implement
    - ☐ Applications seem more expensive and business cannot perceive the value

23 Copyrighted material. 2019

Pair Up

Exercise 1: ALM Assessment

24 Copyrighted material. 2019 

Activity: ALM Practice Assessment

Directions:
1. Pair Up.
2. Score each practice from 1-5, 1= weak 5 = strong
3. Total your score.
4. Decide as a pair, what change to the current ALM practice area would have the most positive impact and why.
5. Be prepared to share your answers with the class.

		1	2	3	4	5
1	Architecture and Design					
2	User Experience					
3	Requirements Management					
4	Software Coding Quality					
5	Software Configuration Management					
6	Data Management					
7	Project Management					
8	Deployment and Operations					
9	Quality Assurance and Test					
10	Application Delivery					
Total						

What change to current ALM practices would have the most positive impact?

Why?

Questions

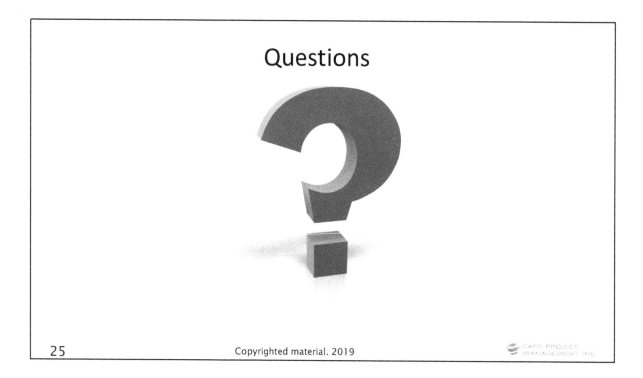

Agile Engineering Overview Extreme Programming (XP)
Module 2

Extreme Programming (XP)

- Developed by Kent Beck
- XP is "a light-weight methodology for small to medium-sized teams developing software in the face of vague or rapidly changing requirements."
- Alternative to "heavy-weight" software development models (which tend to avoid change and customers)

  - "Extreme Programming turns the conventional software process sideways. Rather than planning, analyzing, and designing for the far-flung future, XP programmers do all of these activities a little at a time throughout development."
    -- IEEE Computer , October 1999

27 Copyrighted material. 2019

Why Extreme?

- XP takes commonsense principles and practices to extreme levels:
- If code reviews are good, we'll review code all the time (pair programming).
- If testing is good, everybody will test all the time (unit testing).
- If design is good, we'll make it part of everybody's daily business (refactoring).
- If integration testing is important, then we'll integrate and test several times a day.
- If short iterations are good, we will make the iterations really, really short – seconds, minutes and hours, not weeks, months and years.

28 Copyrighted material. 2019

Four Basic Activities of XP

- Coding: You code because if you don't code, at the end of the day you haven't done anything.

- Testing: You test because if you don't test, you don't know when you are done coding

- Listening: You listen because if you don't listen you don't know what to code or what to test

- Designing: You design so you can keep coding and testing and listening indefinitely

CAPE PROJECT MANAGEMENT, INC.

Extreme Programming (XP) Practices

XP Practices

Whole Team

Collective Ownership

Coding Standard

Test-Driven Development

Customer Tests

Pair Programming

Refactoring

Planning Game

Continuous Integration

Simple Design

Sustainable Pace

Metaphor

Small Releases

www.XProgramming.com

Key:
Blue Ring – Developer Practices
Green Ring – Dev Team Practices
Red Ring – Whole Team Practices

CAPE PROJECT MANAGEMENT, INC.

XP Engineering and Test Practices

- Simple Design
- Test Driven Development
- Refactoring
- Pair Programming
- Collective Code Ownership
- Continuous Integration
- Coding Standards

Copyrighted material. 2019

Simple Design

- Always use the simplest possible design that gets the job done
- The requirements will change tomorrow, so only do what's needed to meet today's requirements
  - No Big Design Up Front (BDUF)
  - Reduces the overhead
- Ship working functionality faster and get feedback early
- "Do The Simplest Thing That Could Possibly Work"
  - Later use refactoring to change it
- Not too much formal documentation

Copyrighted material. 2019

Emergent Design

"The best architectures, requirements, and designs emerge from self-organizing teams."

- Be top down versus Big Up Front Design (BUFD)
- Understand object-oriented design
- Understand design patterns
- Understand test driven development
- Understand refactoring
- Focus on code quality
- Be willing to change

33   Copyrighted material. 2019   CAPE PROJECT MANAGEMENT, INC.

Emergent Design: Agile Architecture

- The design enables reuse across delivery teams.
- The solutions are built from loosely coupled, highly cohesive components.
- There is common technical infrastructure to IT delivery teams to deploy into.
- All team follows effective, common conventions.
- Forum to discuss issues, investigate new technologies or identify candidate architecture strategies.
- Architecture roadmapping occurs in a rolling wave approach and are updated regularly.

34   Copyrighted material. 2019    CAPE PROJECT MANAGEMENT, INC.

Simple Design – Reality

□ Simple design does not mean "no design"

　◘ It is about establishing priorities

　◘ It's a set of tradeoffs you make

　◘ If something is important for this release and for the whole system, it should be designed well

　◘ Don't lose time to design something you will not use soon!

Emergent Design

"The best architectures, requirements, and designs emerge from self-organizing teams."

□ Be top down versus Big Up Front Design (BUFD)

□ Understand object-oriented design

□ Understand design patterns

□ Understand test driven development

□ Understand refactoring

□ Focus on code quality

□ Be willing to change

Emergent Design: Agile Architecture

- The design enables reuse across delivery teams.
- The solutions are built from loosely coupled, highly cohesive components.
- There is common technical infrastructure to IT delivery teams to deploy into.
- All team follows effective, common conventions.
- Forum to discuss issues, investigate new technologies or identify candidate architecture strategies.
- Architecture roadmapping occurs in a rolling wave approach and are updated regularly.

37   Copyrighted material. 2019

Emergent Design: Databases

- Agile database development is particularly hard because databases contain state and must ensure data integrity. They are harder to upgrade or roll back than the front end of a website and so are more amenable to up-front design than continual refinement.
- Agile database development requires a commitment to simple design, refactoring, and automation.
  https://www.red-gate.com/simple-talk/sql/t-sql-programming/agile-database-development/

38   Copyrighted material. 2019   

Test-driven development

- Test first: before adding a feature, write a test for it
- When the complete test suite passes 100%, the feature is accepted
- Two Test Types:
  - Unit Tests automate testing of functionality as developers write it
  - Acceptance Tests (or Functional Tests) are specified by the customer to test that the overall system is functioning as specified
- Common to many other Agile methods and is considered a methodology in itself

39   Copyrighted material. 2019   CAPE PROJECT MANAGEMENT, INC

Traditional Development vs Test-Driven Development

- Traditional Development

- Test-Driven Development

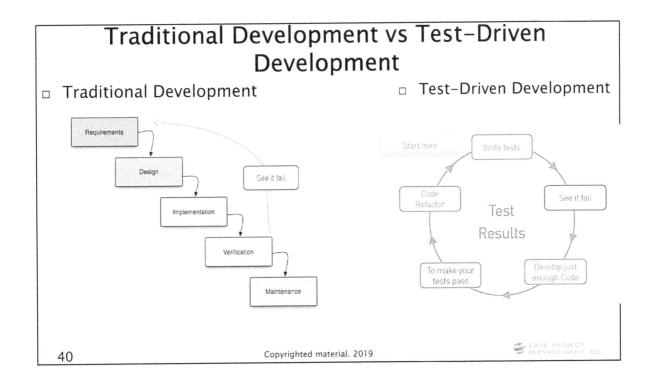

40   Copyrighted material. 2019   CAPE PROJECT MANAGEMENT, INC

Test-Driven Development (TDD)

- Test first development includes continuous design
  - Assumes a design as-you-go approach
- Write automated test
- Run the test
- Build the code
- Run the test
- Refactor
- Repeat

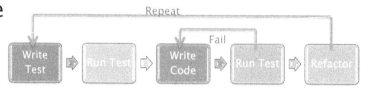

 CAPE PROJECT MANAGEMENT, INC.

Unit Testing/TDD Introduction

- Unit Testing allows you to build the code in small steps, where each step is the simplest thing that can possibly work
- Tests drive the implementation
- Write code from the perspective of consumer of your code
- Leads to precise and required code
- Helps iterative development and emergent design
- Produces testable, self-validating software with regression suite
- Inspires confidence
- Helps bring new developer up to speed

 CAPE PROJECT MANAGEMENT, INC.

The Science of TDD

The evidence says:

- TDD can reduce bug density
- TDD can encourage more modular designs (enhancing software agility/team velocity)
- TDD can reduce code complexity

TDD Best Practices

Unit Tests:

- Should Be Fast: Should be fast in order to execute often (milliseconds)
- Should Be Isolated: Clear where the failures happened. No dependencies between tests. No assumed initial state, nothing left behind
- Should Be Order Agnostic
- Should Be Repeatable: No intermittent behavior. Not dependent on external resources that might not be available
- Should Be Self Validating: No manual interpretation needed, it either passed or failed

TDD Best Practices

- Defect Driven Testing (DDT)
  - Write a unit test that reproduces the defect before fixing the code (most likely it represents missed requirements or boundary conditions)
- Design for Testability
  - Clean Code
  - Separate Construction from Runtime
  - Complexity of Tests Reflect Complexity of Code
- Good Tests Make Excellent Documentation
  - Describes how to use code and is always current
- Unit Tests Methods Show Whole Truth
  - Unit test method shows all parts needed for the test. Avoid use of SetUp methods or Base class that hide the implementation

45

Test-driven development – Reality

- TDD is good for most projects, not for all
  - The real world is different: you always need the functionality "for tomorrow"

- Use unit testing for complex logic only
  - Testing simple logic is overhead

46

TDD and Emergent Design

- Helps tame Speculative Generality
  - "just in case" design/implementation to support anticipated future features that never get implemented (YAGNI, KISS)
- Handles Ambiguity – Encourages the process of decomposing complex requirements into testable specifications
  - Promotes discussion and collaboration
  - Encourages good design principles and practices
- Helps produce good design incrementally
  - Helps stay focused on problem at hand
  - The design emerges as it continuously improves with our improved understanding of the problem domain
- Emergent design assumes change is cheap
  - Removes the fear of refactoring to improve the design (thanks to robust regression suite)

47   Copyrighted material. 2019

GROUP EXERCISE

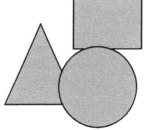

Exercise 2:
Test Driven Development

https://www.tastycupcakes.org/2012/11/tdd-test-driven-drawing/

48   Copyrighted material. 2019

Refactoring

- Refactoring, as originally defined by Martin Fowler and Kent Beck, is: "A change made to the internal structure of software to make it easier to understand and cheaper to modify without changing its observable behavior."
- Refactor mercilessly to keep the design simple
- Keep your code clean and concise, it will be easier to understand, modify, and extend.
- Make sure everything is expressed once and only once.

49   Copyrighted material. 2019

Refactoring

- *...is a disciplined technique for restructuring an existing body of code, altering its internal structure without changing its external behavior.*

50   Copyrighted material. 2019

Why Refactor?

- To make the code base manageable
- To improve the design of the software
- Makes it easy to absorb new changes
- Make the code reusable and concise

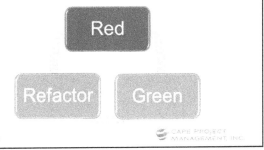

51 Copyrighted material. 2019

Refactoring

□ Refactoring is performed:
  ◘ To fill in short-cuts
  ◘ To eliminate duplication and dead code
  ◘ To make the design and logic clear
  ◘ To make better and clearer use of the programming language
  ◘ To simplify the code and to make it easier to understand
  ◘ To make it easier and safer to change in the future
□ Advantages
  ◘ Enables better understanding and
  ◘ Easier maintenance of code
  ◘ Enables evolving the code slowly over time

52 Copyrighted material. 2019

Technical Debt

☐ Development decisions made in the short term which cause more work in the long-term

☐ Not necessarily apparent to the user

☐ Difficult to measure because the code meets test cases and is not a defect

☐ Major challenge of Agile

☐ The higher the technical debt means the lower the intrinsic quality of the product

☐ Product Owner can work with the Development Team to reduce technical debt by improving the Definition of Done.

53   Copyrighted material. 2019    CAPE PROJECT
MANAGEMENT, INC.

Technical Debt

	Reckless	Prudent
	"We don't have time for design"	"We must ship now and deal with consequences"
Deliberate		
Inadvertent		
	"What's Layering?"	"Now we know how we should have done it"

https://martinfowler.com/bliki/TechnicalDebtQuadrant.html

54   Copyrighted material. 2019    CAPE PROJECT
MANAGEMENT, INC.

Refactoring – Reality

- Delivering working software faster is important
  - Balance writing the code fast versus writing it perfect
    - With simple design
    - With less effort
  - Later you can refactor the code if necessary
- Refactoring is not a reason to intentionally write bad code
  - Good coding style is always important!

Pair Programming

- Two programmers collaborate on the same design, algorithm, code or test case
- Two or more people work together on a single activity
- Follows the principle of "Two heads are better than one"
- Research results:
  - Pair programming increases productivity
  - Higher quality code (15% fewer defects) in about half the time (58%)

Pair Programming

- Two people sit together on the single workstation
- One person writes the code, the other looks "over the shoulder" to provide ideas and ensures code follows the development conventions (Driver and Navigator)
- Pair programmers shift roles on a regular basis
- Advantages:
  - Increases quality
  - Increases skill and knowledge sharing
  - Improves team cohesion
  - Reduces the need for documentation
  - Twice the productivity

Copyrighted material. 2019

 **Pair Up**

Exercise 3: Pair Programming

Microsoft
verPoint Presentat

https://www.industriallogic.com/blog/pairdraw-2/

Pair Programming–Reality

- Pair programming is great for complex and critical logic
  - When developers need good concentration
  - Where quality is really important
  - Especially during design
- Trivial tasks can be done alone
- Peer reviews instead pair programming is often alternative

Collective Code Ownership

- Any team member may add to the code at any time
- Everybody takes responsibility for the whole system
- Encourages simplicity:
  - Prevents complex code from entering the system
- Increases individual responsibility and personal power
- Reduces project risk:
  - Spreads knowledge of the system around the team

Collective Code Ownership – Reality

- Collective code ownership is critical
- Don't allow somebody to own modules and be irreplaceable
- No need to wait for someone else to fix something

Copyrighted material. 2019

Continuous Integration

- Fully automated build and test process
- Allows the team to build and test software many times a day
- XP rule – minimum daily builds
- Eliminates siloed approach to development
- Raises defects immediately
- Creates high-quality code

Copyrighted material. 2019

Continuous Integration

- Code is integrated and tested after a few hours
- Daily builds are not enough:
  - Build, end-to-end, at every check-in
  - Check in frequently
  - Put resources on speeding build time
  - Put resources on speeding test time
- Reduces project risk:
  - You'll never spend days chasing a bug that was created some time in the last few weeks

Continuous Integration (CI) Overview

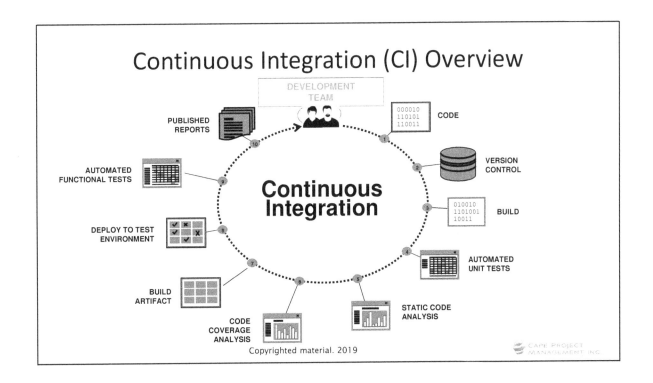

Continuous Integration Dependencies

- Maintain a single source code repository
- Automate the build process
- Automate testing
- Commit as a team to frequent builds
- Develop accurate version control
- Ensure test environment is true mirror of production

Continuous Integration – Reality

- **Integrating often is really valuable**
  - Sometimes you cannot finish a task for one day and integrate it
  - For small projects with small teams integration is not an issue
  - For large and complex projects it's crucial
- **Dependent on an automated build environment**

Coding Standards

□ Programmers write all code in accordance with rules adopted voluntarily by the team

□ Ideally, you should not be able to tell who on the team has touched a specific piece of code

□ Typical Constraints
  ◘ No duplicate code
  ◘ System should have the fewest possible classes
  ◘ System should have the fewest possible methods
  ◘ Comments should be minimized

67   Copyrighted material. 2019

Clean Code

From the Foreword of Clean Code Book

Attentiveness to detail is an even more critical foundation of professionalism than is any grand vision. First, it is through practice in the small that professionals gain proficiency and trust for practice in the large. Second, the smallest bit of sloppy construction of the door that does not close tightly or the slightly crooked tile on the floor, completely dispels the charm of the whole.

That is what clean code is about

68   Copyrighted material. 2019

Common Code Smells

- Duplicate code
- Class design does not follow single responsibility principle (SRP)
- Complex and long method
- Naming conventions not followed for class, method and variables
- Long parameter list

Quality Code Practices

- SOLID Principles
  - SRP – Single Responsibility Principle
  - OCP – Open / Closed Principle
  - LSP – Liskov Substitution Principle
  - ISP – Interface Segregation Principle
  - DIP – Dependency Inversion Principle
- DRY – Don't Repeat Yourself
- YAGNI – You Aren't Gonna Need It
- KISS – Keep It Simple, Stupid

SRP – Single Responsibility Principle

> *"The Single Responsibility Principle states that every object should have a single responsibility, and that responsibility should be entirely encapsulated by the class."*
>
> **Wikipedia**

> *"There should never be more than one reason for a class to change (more than one responsibility)."*
>
> **Robert C. Martin "Uncle Bob"**

Copyrighted material. 2019

OCP – Open / Closed Principle

> *"The Open / Closed Principle states that software entities (classes, modules, functions, etc.) should be open for extension, but closed for modification."*
>
> **Wikipedia**

- ☐ Open to extension
  - ◘ New behavior can be added later
- ☐ Closed to modification
  - ◘ Changes to source or binary code are not required

Copyrighted material. 2019

LSP – Liskov Substitution Principle

> *"The Liskov Substitution Principle* states that subtypes must be substitutable for their base types."*
>
> **Agile Principles, Patterns, and Practices in C#**

- Substitutability – child classes must not:
  - Remove parent class behavior
  - Violate parent class intent

* LSP comes from MIT professor Barbara Liskov

73 Copyrighted material. 2019

ISP – Interface Segregation Principle

> *"The Interface Segregation Principle states that Clients should not be forced to depend on methods they do not use."*
>
> **Agile Principles, Patterns, and Practices in C#**

- Segregate interfaces
  - Prefer small, cohesive interfaces
  - Divide "fat" interfaces into smaller ones

74 Copyrighted material. 2019

DIP – Dependency Inversion Principle

> *"Dependency Inversion Principle says that high-level modules should not depend on low-level modules. Both should depend on abstractions."*
>
> *"Abstractions should not depend on details. Details should depend on abstractions."*
>
> **Agile Principles, Patterns, and Practices in C#**

- Goal: decoupling between modules through abstractions
  - Programming through interfaces

75   Copyrighted material. 2019

Don't Repeat Yourself (DRY) Principle

> *"Every piece of knowledge must have a single, unambiguous representation in the system."*
>
> **The Pragmatic Programmer**

> *"Repetition in logic calls for abstraction. Repetition in process calls for automation."*
>
> **97 Things Every Programmer Should Know**

- DRY principle variations:
  - Once and Only Once (OOO)
  - Duplication Is Evil (DIE)

76   Copyrighted material. 2019

YAGNI – You Aren't Gonna Need It

> *"A programmer should not add functionality until deemed necessary."*
>
> **Wikipedia**

> *"Always implement things when you actually need them, never when you just foresee that you need them."*
>
> **Ron Jeffries, XP co-founder**

Copyrighted material. 2019  CAPE PROJECT MANAGEMENT, INC.

KISS – Keep It Simple, Stupid

> *"Most systems work best if they are kept simple."*
>
> **U.S. Navy**

> *"Simplicity should be a key goal in design and unnecessary complexity should be avoided."*
>
> **Wikipedia**

Copyrighted material. 2019  CAPE PROJECT MANAGEMENT, INC.

Coding Standards – Reality

- Coding standards are important
  - Enforce good practices to whole the team – tools, code reviews, etc.
- Standards should be simple and concise
  - Complex standards are not followed
  - Standards should be more strict for larger teams
  - No broad rules like "comment any class member"

Static and Dynamic Code Analysis

- Static Analysis tools look for defects in code
  - Problems such as security defects or coding style issues
  - Provides a quick visibility into the quality of the code.
  - Various tools available for automated static analysis on code
- Static Code Analysis should be used:
  - As a part of the team's "Continuous Integration" efforts
  - In Outsourced projects
  - In Regulatory Compliance Situations
- Dynamic Code Analysis
  - involves examining the executed code to find out problems and failures
- Both Static and Dynamic Code Analysis is essential especially when teams are geographically distributed

Activity: XP Practices

Directions:
1. Pair up with someone
2. Review the XP practices
3. Identify Strengths and Weakness
4. As a pair, select 2 practices which would have the biggest impact on your engineering Agility
5. Be prepared to share your answers with the class.

XP Practice	Strength	Weakness	Biggest Impact?
1. Simple Design			
2. Test Driven Development			
3. Refactoring			
4. Pair Programming			
5. Collective Code Ownership			
6. Continuous Integration			
7. Coding Standards			

Pair Up

Exercise 4: XP Assessment

Questions

Agile Test Strategies

Module 3

DISCUSSION

Define Quality

84

Definition of Quality

□ Quality is:

◻ "The totality of features and characteristics of a product or service that bears on its ability to satisfy given needs."

Source: ANSI/ASQC, 1978

85

CAPE PROJECT
MANAGEMENT, INC

Agile vs. Traditional Quality Management

Traditional Quality Management	Agile Quality Management
▶ Conformance to requirements	▶ Fitness for Use
▶ Focus on delivery of software meeting contractual specification	▶ Want to Satisfy the Customer
▶ Requirements may not fully represent customer expectations	▶ Focus on Delivery of Valuable Software
▶ Documentation is a critical aspect of quality management	▶ Values Working software over comprehensive documentation
▶ More aligned to Crosby's interpretation of quality	▶ More in alignment with Juran's Definition of Quality

86

CAPE PROJECT
MANAGEMENT, INC

Focus on Value

The Traditional Iron Triangle

The Agile Triangle

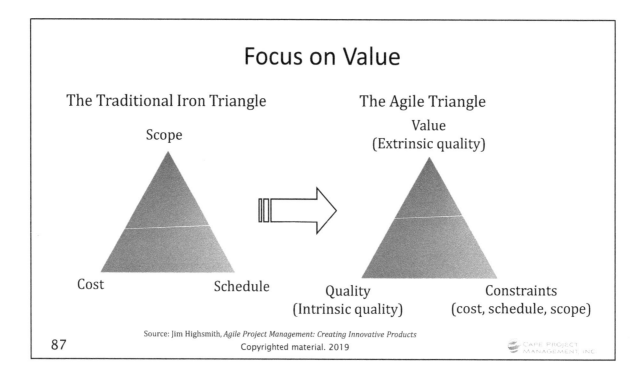

Scope

Cost

Schedule

Value
(Extrinsic quality)

Quality
(Intrinsic quality)

Constraints
(cost, schedule, scope)

Source: Jim Highsmith, *Agile Project Management: Creating Innovative Products*
Copyrighted material. 2019

87

Intrinsic versus Extrinsic Quality

- Intrinsic Quality is all of the qualities that are built into the product: suitability, durability, reliability, uniformity, and maintainability. This type of quality can be measured quantitatively such as test coverage, bugs per line of code, escaped defects, cohesion, etc.

- Extrinsic Quality is the buyer's perception of quality and the value to the customer. This is a more qualitative measurement based upon sales and customer feedback.

Source: Joseph Kelada, *Integrating Reengineering with Total Quality*

88

Copyrighted material. 2019

DISCUSSION

Risks in Traditional Testing

Copyrighted material. 2019

Challenges of Traditional Testing

- □ Large volumes of manual test activities slow down delivery.
- □ Teams put off testing until the end of projects, squeezing it in the process.
- □ Late-breaking defects can derail projects.
- □ Developers only see the results of poor quality in retrospect, when the consequences of their actions are harder and more costly to fix.

Copyrighted material. 2019

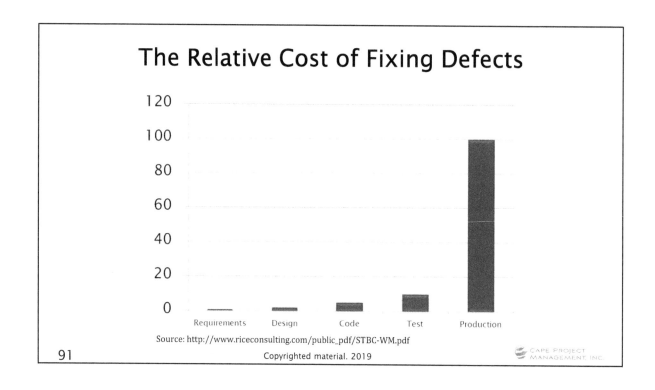

Source: http://www.riceconsulting.com/public_pdf/STBC-WM.pdf

Copyrighted material. 2019

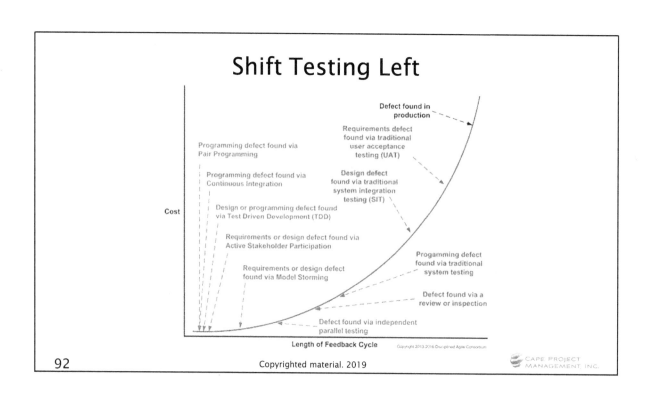

Copyrighted material. 2019

Benefits of Agile Testing

- On-going feedback to developers allows testers to ask the right questions at the right time.
- Early identification of dependencies, technical or testing challenges and roadblocks.
- Embraces change as a healthy and real part of software development.
- Team collaboration helps everyone work together toward a common goal.
- Quality comes first because final acceptance criteria are established prior to the work beginning.

GROUP EXERCISE

Exercise 5: The Testing Manifesto

https://leanpub.com/AgileTesting/read

49

The Testing Manifesto

Source http://www.growingagile.co.za/2015/04/the-testing-manifesto/

95 Copyrighted material. 2019

Agile Quality Assurance & Control

- Product Owner/Customer in the Team
  - Software that meets the Product Owner's intent
  - Product Owner is the single owner of quality and becomes part of the team and guides development.
- Releasable Software in every Timebox, which:
  - Meets the Product Owner's expectations
  - Adheres to a Definition of Done
  - Has to best design for the currently implemented features (via refactoring)
  - Is easily maintainable (via refactoring)
  - Has been tested to the satisfaction of the team and relevant stakeholders
  - Is value-driven
- Iterative and Continuous Product Reviews
  - Results are documented and incorporated into backlog
  - Defects are managed as backlog items
  - Technical debt is more prevalent on Agile teams

96 Copyrighted material. 2019

Additional Quality Best Practices

- The Role of the Tester
- Whole Team
- Parallel Teams
- Real Time Defect Management
- Agile Test Environments
- Acceptance Test Driven Development (ATDD)
- Reviews and Inspections
- Exploratory Testing
- Hardening Iterations
- More...

Role of an Agile Tester

- Testers are integral part of the team
- Participate in Release/Iteration planning
- Start testing activities from the day 1
- Collaborates with the customer to define the acceptance test criteria
- Validates that the system is doing exactly what it is supposed to do
- Tests Stories once they are complete
- Focuses on test automation
- Focuses more on exploratory testing
- Practices pair testing (similar to pair programming)
- Collaborates with Development team
- Provides continuous feedback to the team

Development Team Testing Strategies

☐ Agile teams generally follow "Whole Team" strategy where people with testing skills are "embedded" effectively into development teams

☐ Independent parallel testing teams are used in certain situations

Copyrighted material. 2019

The Whole Team Strategy

☐ Important Constructs of Whole Team Strategy:
- ☐ Team to include the right people so that they have the requisite skills
- ☐ Team has a balanced perspective required for the team to succeed.
- ☐ Focuses on successful delivery a working system on a regular basis
- ☐ All contribute in any way they can, thereby increasing the overall productivity.
- ☐ Quicker Feedback Cycles

☐ Resulting Approach
- ☐ Testers are "embedded" in the development team
- ☐ Testers actively participate in all aspects of the project

☐ Weaknesses of this Approach
- ☐ Group Think
- ☐ Team may not have all the needed skills
- ☐ Team may not know what skills are needed

Copyrighted material. 2019

The Independent Test Team

- Possible Criteria for Choosing Independent Test Team
  - Teams in complex environments
  - Teams in regulatory compliance situations
  - Need to supplement their whole team
  - Different geographies and time zones
- Activities done
  - Test team will perform parallel independent testing throughout the project
  - Responsible for the end-of-lifecycle testing performed during the release/transition phase
- The goal of these efforts is
  - To supplements the "Whole Team" approach
  - To find out where the system breaks
  - Report such breakages so that development team can fix them.

Regression Testing

- Regression testing is testing done to check that a update do not re-introduce errors that have been corrected earlier or create new errors.
  - High-performing Agile teams perform all regression testing via automated testing to support rapid releases
  - Independent test teams are used when automation does not exist or does not have enough coverage
  - Limit manual testing to high-priority use cases

Real-Time Defect Management

- Defect Management in Agile Projects is simpler than in Traditional Projects
- In the Whole Team approach, once the defect is found, it is fixed on the spot
- Here the entire defect management process is through conversations between people
- When independent test teams are present, then defect tracking tools can be used.

Copyrighted material. 2019

Testing Environment Set Up

- Suggestions for Test Environment Strategy
  - Adopt open source software for developers
  - Adopt commercial tools for independent testers
  - Have a shared bug/defect tracking system
  - Invest in testing hardware including simulated production environments
  - Invest in virtualization and test lab management tools
  - Invest in continuous integration & continuous deployment tools

Copyrighted material. 2019

Managing Test Data

- Managing test data is critical and necessary for having a good test suite
- An application can use data from numerous sources like database, external sources, stubbed data manager
- Keep data up-to-date is important to make your test effective
- Data can be available in different formats like CSV, XML, JSON, etc
- Generic utilities and tools can be built to minimize redundant tasks

Acceptance Test Driven Development

- □ Discuss the Requirements: Solicit acceptance criteria from stakeholders
- □ Distill Tests: Modify the test plans to fit in automated testing framework
- □ Develop the Code: Connect the test to the code
- □ Implementing Code: Run the tests against the code
- □ Demo the tests: Use exploratory testing to try new scenarios

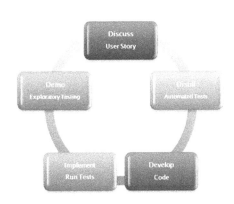

Acceptance Criteria

- Acceptance criteria define the boundaries of a User Story, and are used to confirm when a story is completed and working as intended.
- The tests are written before development
- They are ideally created by the Product Owner
- Does not replace unit tests
- Often written on the back of the User Story card

Copyrighted material. 2019

Why use Acceptance Tests?

- They get the team to think through how a feature or piece of functionality will work from the user's perspective
- They remove ambiguity from requirements
- They form the tests that will confirm that a feature or piece of functionality is working and complete.

Copyrighted material. 2019

Acceptance Tests

- Simple version
  - Customer writes the acceptance tests with help from the developer and the user stories
  - Developers write code to make the acceptance tests pass, reports results to the customer
- Using an acceptance test framework
  - Customers write acceptance tests in some format (e.g. fill in tables in a spreadsheet)
  - Framework maps tests to code stubs that will perform the tests
  - Developer fills in the code for the framework that will perform the actual tests
  - Upon running tests the framework automatically maps the results to a format for the customer to understand (e.g. HTML)
  - Framework makes it easier to run regression tests, allow the customer to track progress

Sample Acceptance Test

- Writing cash register software
- Acceptance Test: Shopping cart for generating a receipt
  - Create a shopping cart with:
    - 1 lb. coffee, 3 bags of cough drops, 1 gallon milk
    - Prices: Coffee $6/lb, cough drops $2.49/bag, milk $4.95/gallon
    - Verify total is $18.42
- Test might span multiple stories (fill shopping cart, checkout, view receipt...)
- Other tests might verify sales tax is calculated correctly, coupons properly discounted, etc.
- Not comprehensive tests, but specific cases to test user stories and functionality

Running Acceptance Tests

☐ You can run them manually, such as through a GUI interface
- Select milk from the drop down menu
- Enter 1 and Click on "add" button
- Select coffee from the drop down menu
- Enter 1 and Click on "add" button
- Select cough drops from the drop down menu
- Enter 3 and Click on "add" button
- Verify shopping cart subtotal displays $18.42

☐ Useful to run but can be time consuming, and should be automated for regression testing

111   Copyrighted material. 2019

Acceptance Tests are Important

☐ Gives customer some satisfaction that features are correctly implemented

☐ Not the same as Unit Test
- Unit tests could pass but acceptance tests fail, especially if acceptance test requires the integration of components that were unit-tested

112   Copyrighted material. 2019

Reviews and Inspections

- Review is a validation technique in which artifacts are examined critically by one or more people (generally peers)
- Basic Constructs
  - Get a group of people evaluate an artifact, (code, requirements, user stories etc.) in an environment (formal or informal) to determine if the artifact is of sufficient quality
  - It indicates mistakes early in the lifecycle
  - Has a short feedback cycle
- Involves many types
  - Code Walkthroughs
  - Peer Reviews
  - Formal Inspection

113   Copyrighted material. 2019

Reviews

- Sprint Review
  - Reviews are done at the end of every Sprint / iteration
  - Goal is to show the explicit progress to key stakeholders
  - Gets feedback from all stakeholders
- All Hands Reviews
  - This involves demonstrating the product for all project stakeholders who work directly or indirectly with the team (and not just the primary stakeholders)
  - Generally done prior to a release
  - This is primarily done for:
    - Gain confidence of the stakeholders
    - Get feedback

114   Copyrighted material. 2019

Exploratory Testing

- Unscripted testing where testers generally explore the application's functionality without restraint
- Encourage testers to plan as they test and to use information gathered during testing to affect the actual way testing is performed
- Often occurs after the iteration in the period between "done" and "done-done."
- Always performed in conjunction with traditional testing

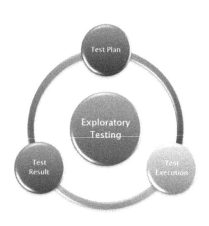

Test Doubles

A generic term for any kind of pretend object used in place of a real object for testing purposes.

- **Dummy** objects are passed around but never actually used. Usually they are just used to fill parameter lists.
- **Test Stubs** provide canned answers to calls made during the test, usually not responding at all to anything outside what's programmed in for the test.
- **Test Spies** are stubs that also record some information based on how they were called.
- **Fake objects** actually have working implementations, but usually take some shortcut which makes them not suitable for production
- **Mock objects** are objects pre-programmed with expectations which form a specification of the calls they are expected to receive.
  - Of these kinds of doubles, only mocks insist upon behavior verification.

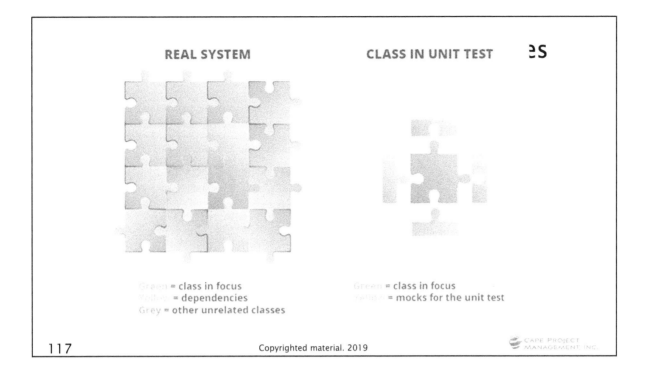

REAL SYSTEM   CLASS IN UNIT TEST   2s

Green = class in focus
Yellow = dependencies
Grey = other unrelated classes

Green = class in focus
Yellow = mocks for the unit test

Copyrighted material. 2019

Mocking Why?

- To test in isolation
- To test at a micro level
- Sometimes, only interfaces exist, implementations are not even coded
- "Real" objects required in unit tests are hard to instantiate or configure
- Enables behavior and interaction testing
  - Did my controller invoked the service correctly?
  - Did my service invoked the DAO correctly?
- Not dependent on external resources – database, filesystem
- Test a single responsibility for a method

Copyrighted material. 2019

Mock Frameworks

Mocking Best Practices

- Right balance needs to be drawn between state vs behavior testing
- Mocking everything will make the test less powerful

State vs. Behavior testing

- State testing checks the state of a property of an object. Assertion is done to validate the actual with the expected
  - assertThat(ball.getColor(), is('red'));
  - assertThat(list.size(), is(4));
- Behavior testing verifies the behavior of an object in relation to the invocation made
  - verify(mock, never()).someMethod("never called");
  - verify(mock, atLeastOnce()).someMethod("called at least once");
  - verify(mock, atLeast(2)).someMethod("called at least twice");
  - verify(mock, times(5)).someMethod("called five times");
  - verify(mock, atMost(3)).someMethod("called at most 3 times");

121

CAPE PROJECT MANAGEMENT, INC.

How Agile Teams Validate Their Work

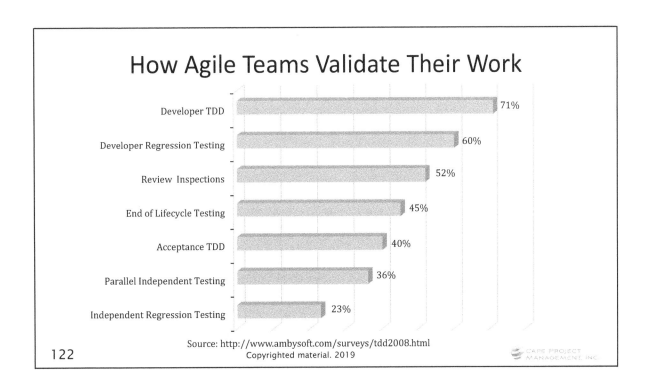

Source: http://www.ambysoft.com/surveys/tdd2008.html

122

CAPE PROJECT MANAGEMENT, INC.

Activity: Agile Testing Assessment

Directions:

1. Pair-up with another person at your table review the list of Agile Testing Strategies
2. Score each strategy on a scale for 1-5. 1= Never, 5=All the time

Principle	Testing Maturity 1-5
Whole Team	
Real Time Defect Management	
Unit Testing	
Automated Testing	
Code Reviews	
Acceptance Test Driven Development (ATDD)	
Stakeholder Reviews and Inspections	
Exploratory Testing	
Total	

Pair Up

Exercise 6: Agile Testing Assessment

123

Questions

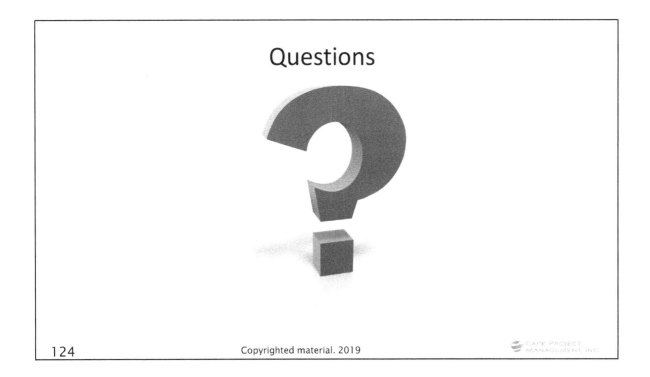

124

Lifecycle Testing

Module 4

Overview

- Agile testing is all about applying Agile values and principles to testing. The value of Agile testing lies in effective communication between developers, testers and the Product Owner
- Need to understand three paradigms
  - When to test
  - How to test
  - How much to test
- In the end a story is not "Done" until testing is finished.

Agile Testing Context

- Testing is no longer a separate phase in Agile projects
- Testing activities are performed by cross functional team members when possible
- Testers commit to tasks as part of Scrum team in Sprint planning
- Plan for current iteration only
- Along with user stories, testers need to understand acceptance criteria
- Adhere to a complete Definition of Done

127   Copyrighted material. 2019

Agile Test Planning

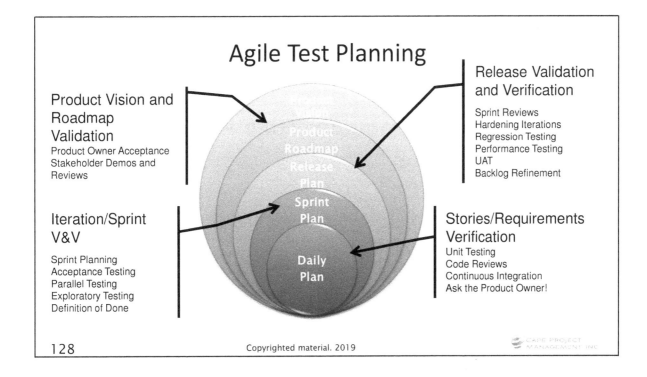

Product Vision and Roadmap Validation
Product Owner Acceptance
Stakeholder Demos and Reviews

Release Validation and Verification
Sprint Reviews
Hardening Iterations
Regression Testing
Performance Testing
UAT
Backlog Refinement

Iteration/Sprint V&V
Sprint Planning
Acceptance Testing
Parallel Testing
Exploratory Testing
Definition of Done

Stories/Requirements Verification
Unit Testing
Code Reviews
Continuous Integration
Ask the Product Owner!

128   Copyrighted material. 2019

Success Factors

- Automate tests
  - Automate tests wherever practical
  - Need rapid feedback
- Collaborate
  - Collaborate with customers
  - Collaborate with team
- Continually improve
  - Participate in retrospectives
  - Personal training

- Testers are part of the team:
  - Collective ownership
- Agile Testing Mindset
  - Drop the "Quality Police" mindset
  - Not trying to break the system, but trying to build a better system
  - Focus on team goals & customer value

Focus Areas

- High Value features first
- Continuous Integration with pre/post release build automation
- Test Driven development
- Automation of unit & regression testing
- Automated acceptance testing
- Exploratory testing

Philosophy

- Agile Test Philosophy:
  - Test Early
  - Test Often
  - Test Enough
- Test Process
  - Analyze a little
  - Design a little
  - Code a little
  - Test what you can

Agile Test Planning

- Agile test plans
  - Upfront, high level plan
  - Detailed incremental plans
- Upfront test planning activities
  - Specify test environment
  - Procedures for using the test environment
  - System test policies and procedures
  - System test objectives and scope
  - Determine staffing requirements and responsibilities
  - Decide on tools to be used
  - Scheduling and other management activities
    - Define system test tasks, schedule, and timelines
    - Perform risk analysis for the test activities

Documentation

- Minimal documentation is key
- Agile encourages and mandates:
  - Interwoven team
  - Discussions
  - Collaboration
  - Simplified Documents
  - Evolving Documents
- Enables and helps in:
  - Less Documentation Effort
  - Less Formal Paper Work
  - Easy to Understand Requirements
  - High Productivity due to high involvement
  - Low number of unknown defects (hopefully!)

Copyrighted material. 2019  CAPE PROJECT MANAGEMENT, INC.

Good Enough Artifacts

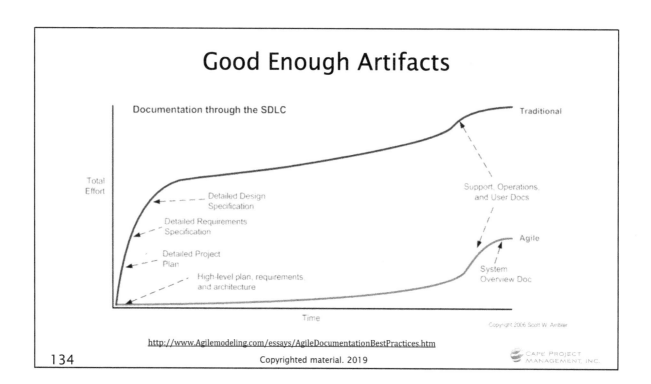

http://www.Agilemodeling.com/essays/AgileDocumentationBestPractices.htm

Copyrighted material. 2019

Planning for a Release

- ☐ Ownership of the activity
  - ☐ Product owner is the primary owner
  - ☐ Inputs are solicited from other team members collaboratively
- ☐ Important Factors for Planning a Release
  - ☐ Expectations & Needs of Product Owner
  - ☐ Specific abilities and other testing requirements
  - ☐ Independence & Autonomy
  - ☐ Infrastructure
  - ☐ Tools & Automation
  - ☐ Major Risks and Mitigations

Iterative Test Planning

- ☐ For every iteration, testers should:
  - ☐ Provide inputs for planning.
  - ☐ Provide an estimate for the testing effort
  - ☐ Verify that the developers have included adequate time for unit testing in their estimates
  - ☐ Ensure that necessary resources are in place for this increment
- ☐ Preferred release in frequent small releases (incremental deployment)
  - ☐ Very good for the development team
  - ☐ Necessary for the client to gain confidence

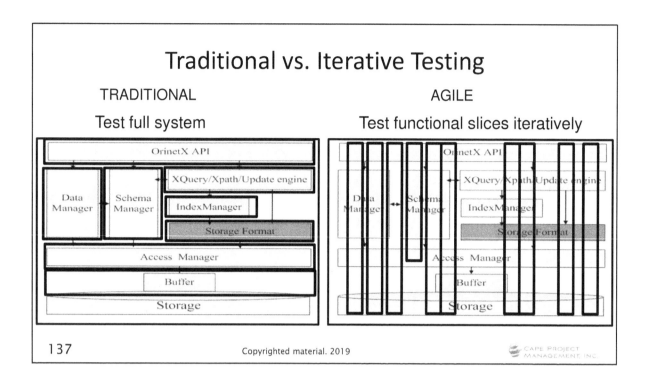

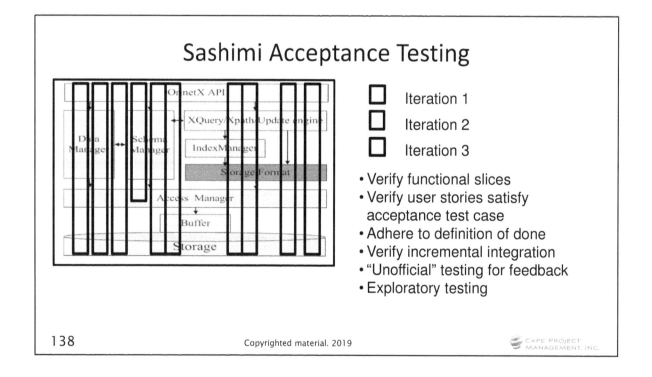

Sashimi Acceptance Testing

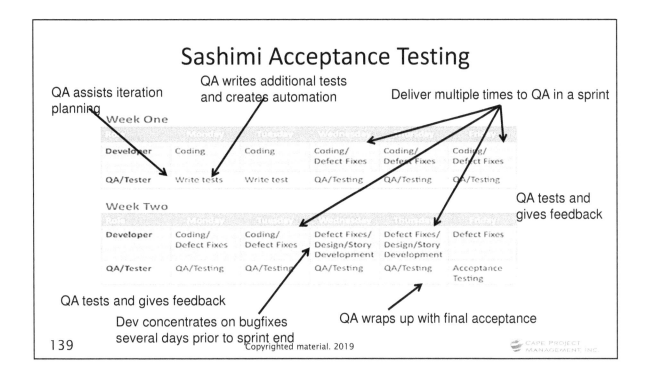

QA assists iteration planning

QA writes additional tests and creates automation

Deliver multiple times to QA in a sprint

QA tests and gives feedback

QA tests and gives feedback

Dev concentrates on bugfixes several days prior to sprint end

QA wraps up with final acceptance

139

CAPE PROJECT MANAGEMENT, INC.

Regression Testing

- Iterative development accommodates the following by design
  - Constant change in feature set
  - Constant change in expectations of the stakeholders
  - Constant prototyping
  - Continuous enhancement of the required features
- Regression, becomes naturally an important activity
  - Incremental design and refactoring requires extensive regression testing
  - Frequent regression testing necessitates automation
- Unit and acceptance testing proceeds in parallel

140

CAPE PROJECT MANAGEMENT, INC.

Regression Testing

- Subset (or all) can be executed nightly as CI build test
- Integration of previous releases and sprints
- Comprehensive, thorough verification
- Identify "lost" fixes and new issues
- Automated tests to expose bugs that were previously fixed – in case they return
- Automated tests of new sprint functionality

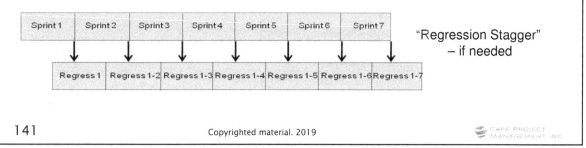

"Regression Stagger"
– if needed

Copyrighted material. 2019

CAPE PROJECT
MANAGEMENT INC.

Performance Testing

- ☐ Like regression testing, it should be performed as close to the time of development as possible.
- ☐ Typical volume test objectives:
  - ◻ Test to check if there is any data loss
  - ◻ Check the system's response time
  - ◻ Check if the data is stored correctly or not
  - ◻ Verify if the data is overwritten without any notification
  - ◻ Check for warning and error messages, whether it comes at all for volume problems
  - ◻ Check whether high volume data affects the speed of processing

Copyrighted material. 2019

CAPE PROJECT
MANAGEMENT INC.

Independent Team Test Design

- Test Design Activities
  - Defining test scenarios based upon Themes, Epics and User Stories
  - Identifying test cases including input, pre-conditions, output and post-conditions
  - Identifying and creating test data
  - Defining test procedures to conduct each test
  - Modifying existing scripts
  - Determining the detailed order in which tests will be executed
  - Writing and testing programs to load data in the test database, to compare expected results with actual results, to conduct the tests etc.
  - Setting up the test environment

143   Copyrighted material. 2019   

Bugs

- At the end of an increment there should be no known bugs in the delivered code for that increment
  - Stories that don't yet pass all the tests are deferred till a future increment – or split, and only the part that passes all tests is delivered
- Bugs that are discovered during acceptance testing or in the field are placed with new stories
  - The customer decides to fix a bug or add new functionality

144   Copyrighted material. 2019   

Bug Tracking

- Agile teams focus on preventing bugs not finding and tracking them – Ask questions!
- Logging minor issues is waste
- Every issue that is found
  - Fix it immediately (Most of the time)
  - Decide it will never be fixed, so do not log it (occasionally)
  - Write a new story to deal with the issue (Rarely)

Bug Tracking Reporting

Bug Name: Application crash on clicking the SAVE button while creating a new user.
Bug ID: (It will be automatically created by the BUG Tracking tool once you save this bug)
Area Path: USERS menu > New Users
Build Number: Version Number 5.0.1
Severity: (High/Medium/Low) or 1,2,3
Priority: (High/Medium/Low) or 1,2,3
Assigned to: Developer-X
Reported By: Your Name
Reported On: Date
Reason: Defect
Status: New/Open/Active (Depends on the Tool you are using)
Environment: Windows 2003/SQL Server 2005
Description:
Steps to Reproduce:
Expected Result:

End of Lifecycle Testing

- As a part of release effort, "end of lifecycle" testing is done in Agile Projects
- Here an independent team validates that the system is ready to go into production
- Often called Hardening Iterations

Copyrighted material. 2019

Hardening Iterations

- Final exploratory and field testing
- Checklist validation against release, QA and standards governance
- Release signoffs if you need them
- Create operations and support documentation
- Create a deployment package
- Communicate release to everyone
- Show traceability for regulatory compliance

- Also called a "Tail". A long tail reflects broken Agile processes and an incomplete Definition of Done.

Copyrighted material. 2019

Activity: Test Planning

Directions:
1. Get into groups of 3 or 4 and document the components of a typical test plan.
2. Decide which changes you would like to realistically make immediately.
3. Decide which changes you would like to make within the next year.
4. Be prepared to share your answers with the class.

Typical Test Plan:

Near-term changes:

Long-term changes:

GROUP EXERCISE

Exercise 7: Test Planning

149   Copyrighted material. 2019

Questions

150   Copyrighted material. 2019

Non Functional Testing
Module 5

Overview

- Non-functional requirements,
  - Also known as "technical requirements" or "quality of service" (QoS) requirements
  - Primarily focus on aspects that cross cut functional requirements
  - Typically these are system level qualities
  - Span multiple components / products / applications / services
  - Generally can be tested at system level
- Classified into Internal and External Qualities
- Common Non-Functional attributes include:
  - Performance
  - Security
  - Usability
  - Internationalization
  - Reliability
  - Supportability

Technical Requirements

- Written by development team, architect, tech lead
- Don't have to be written as User Stories
- Non-Functional Requirements (NFRs) are often part of the Acceptance Criteria
- They can also be part of the Definition of Done

Prioritizing Technical Requirements

- Projects have to balance delivering features along with doing all the important behind-the-scenes work.
- Leaving non-functional development until very late in the project has two major problems:
  - It costs more
  - It creates project risks that can lead to project problems

Source http://tynerblain.com/blog/2009/02/10/Agile-non-functional-reqs/

Non Functional Requirements

- Overview
  - Considered as "constraints"
  - Impose constraints to guide work
  - Cross-cut functional requirement
  - Reduce functional scope to a scenario
- Two types of Constraints
  - Rule – global
  - Restriction – scenario
- Specifying NFRs
  - Bounded
  - Independent
  - Negotiable
  - Testable

155

NFR Examples

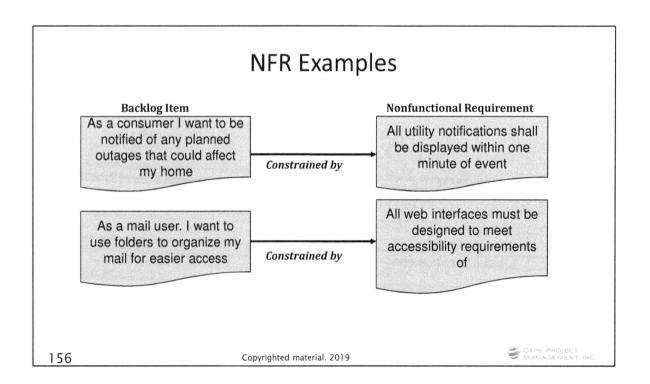

156

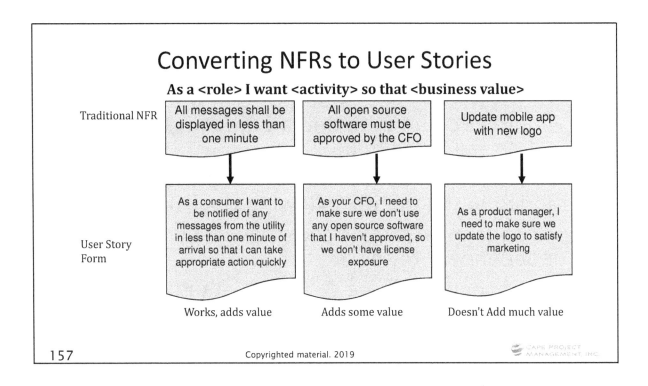

Converting NFRs to User Stories

As a <role> I want <activity> so that <business value>

Traditional NFR	All messages shall be displayed in less than one minute	All open source software must be approved by the CFO	Update mobile app with new logo
User Story Form	As a consumer I want to be notified of any messages from the utility in less than one minute of arrival so that I can take appropriate action quickly	As your CFO, I need to make sure we don't use any open source software that I haven't approved, so we don't have license exposure	As a product manager, I need to make sure we update the logo to satisfy marketing
	Works, adds value	Adds some value	Doesn't Add much value

157

Copyrighted material. 2019

NFRs in Acceptance Criteria

Requirement type	Example
Performance	• The interaction between the user and the system should not exceed 2 seconds. • The system should receive updated information every 15 minutes.
Security	• Only direct managers can see personnel records of staff • Only Finance can see payment information
Cultural & Political	• The system should be able to distinguish between United States and European currency • The system shall comply with industry privacy standards.

158

Copyrighted material. 2019

NFRs in Definition of Done

- The system must support 500 new users signing up and initiating a new user login within the same hour.
- The system must support 10,000 users added in the month following go-live.
- All code must pass a code review by an independent reviewer.
- All UI should adhere to the UX standards in the following wiki...

Strategies for Non Functional Testing

- Independent Parallel Testing
  - Goal is to validate the system built
  - Performed throughout the lifecycle
  - Smaller testing teams focusing on specialized tests
  - Highly skilled specialists
  - Utilizes sophisticated tools and labs
- Developer Education
  - Improve understanding on NFRs and how testing will be performed

Questions

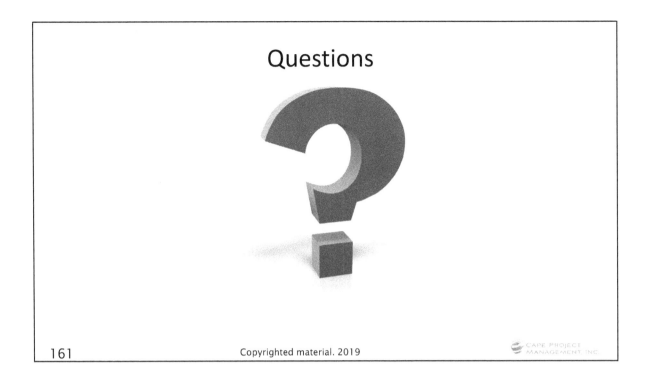

Test Automation in Agile
Module 6

What is Automated Testing?

- Automated testing is any testing that is done without human interaction. Tests can be fully automated, or partially automated.
- Automated tests can take the following forms:
  - Unit Testing
  - Data Setup
  - Installation
  - Test Execution of any type of test – db, web, UI, web service
  - Integration Testing
  - Regression Testing
  - Performance Testing
  - Security & Penetration Testing

163   Copyrighted material. 2019

Why use automated tests?

- Constant communication between testing and development efforts
- Quick visibility into code quality
- Free up time for most important work
- Repeatable
- Safety net
- Quick feedback
- Helps drive coding
- Manual tests are error prone
- Main reason: Automation is often the only way to generate the velocity for testing needed to release fully tested builds and potential shippable projects in short iterations

164   Copyrighted material. 2019   

Agile Test Execution Tools

- Test Generation (data and script generators)
- System configuration
- Simulators
- Test execution (harnesses and test scripts)
- Probes
- Activity recording & coverage analysis
- Test management

Principles Guiding Agile Test Automation

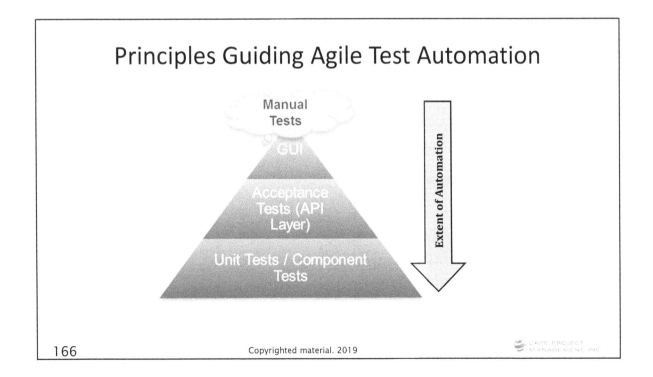

Level 1 – Unit / Component Tests

- ☐ Base of the Pyramid
  - ◘ Unit Test / Component Tests
  - ◘ Essential for a solid automation foundation
  - ◘ Represents the largest part of the pyramid
  - ◘ Provides valuable information to developers
  - ◘ Tests are written in the same language used by developers

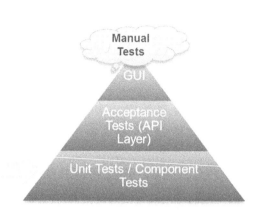

167   Copyrighted material. 2019   CAPE PROJECT MANAGEMENT, INC.

Level 2 – Service Tests

- ☐ Middle of the Pyramid
  - ◘ Acceptance Tests / Service Tests
  - ◘ Generally called Service Layer Testing
  - ◘ Test the services within the application (without using the front end)

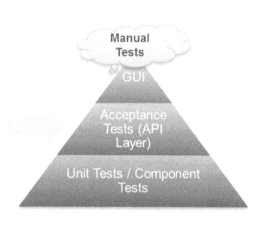

168   Copyrighted material. 2019    CAPE PROJECT MANAGEMENT, INC.

Level 3 – GUI Tests

- Top of the Pyramid
  - GUI Tests
  - Placed at the top of the pyramid
  - GUI testing can be time consuming to create

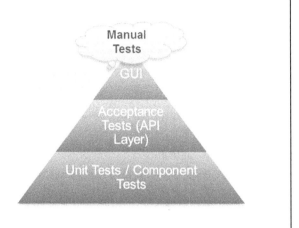

Copyrighted material. 2019

Creating an Automated Test Strategy

- What type of tests needed for the developer to ensure quality
- What business facing tests are needed
- What tests are needed to ensure a Sprint is "Done"
- What tests need to be performed in order to support a release.

Copyrighted material. 2019

Best Practices for Writing Automated Tests

- Best Practices for UI tests:
    - Do not simply record and playback tests
    - Parameterize data use for tests – Data-Driven Testing
    - Parameterize field names for easy maintenance
    - Write reusable modules for common test functions
    - Make tests atomic – tests should not depend on other tests
    - Remember: automated tests are code, and should be planned just like coding for an application
- Do not automate:
    - Usability Tests / Look and Feel tests
    - Customer Ad-hoc tests
    - Exploratory tests
    - Tests that never fail

171   

Testing Tools

Some automated test tools are:

- TestNG –open source unit and integration testing for java
- Selenium IDE/RC – open source automated web testing framework
- soapUI – open source web services/SOA automated testing
- Jmeter/BadBoy – open source load testing for web applications
- Fitnesse – wiki-based automation framework
- Cucumber/Gherkin – runs automated acceptance tests written in a behavior-driven development (BDD) style.
- HP QuickTest Pro, HP WinRunner, HP LoadRunner, HP Performance Center, Rational – commercial tools
- Write your own!

172   

Test Automation Common Mistakes

☐ These are common mistakes teams make about auto-tests:

- ◻ Improper planning
- ◻ Planning for unwanted features
- ◻ Not hiring individuals with right skills in automation
- ◻ Not involving developers while automating

Agile Testing Quadrants

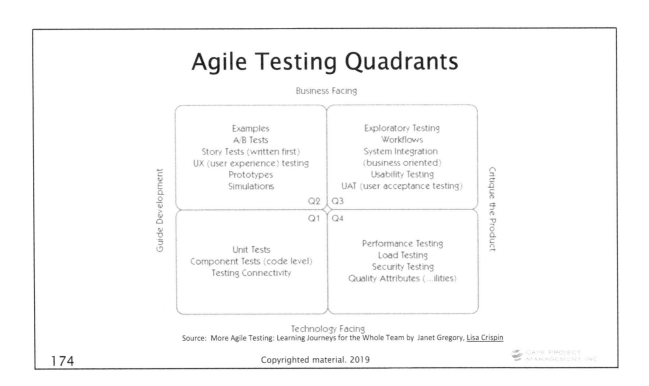

Source: More Agile Testing: Learning Journeys for the Whole Team by Janet Gregory, Lisa Crispin

Directions:

In your groups:

1. Draw the four quadrants on a big sheet of paper or used the attached quadrants.
2. Document within each quadrant which ones you perform and which ones you don't.
3. What's the weakest quadrant? What's your strongest quadrant?
4. What is the easiest thing to address in your weakest quadrant?

Guide Development

Business Facing

Technology Facing

Critique the Product

Q2

Examples
A/B Tests
Story Tests (written first)
UX (user experience) testing
Prototypes
Simulations

Q1

Unit Tests
Component Tests (code level)
Testing Connectivity

Q3

Exploratory Testing
Workflows
System Integration
(business oriented)
Usability Testing
UAT (user acceptance testing)

Q4

Performance Testing
Load Testing
Security Testing
Quality Attributes (...ilities)

Guide Development
(Preventing)

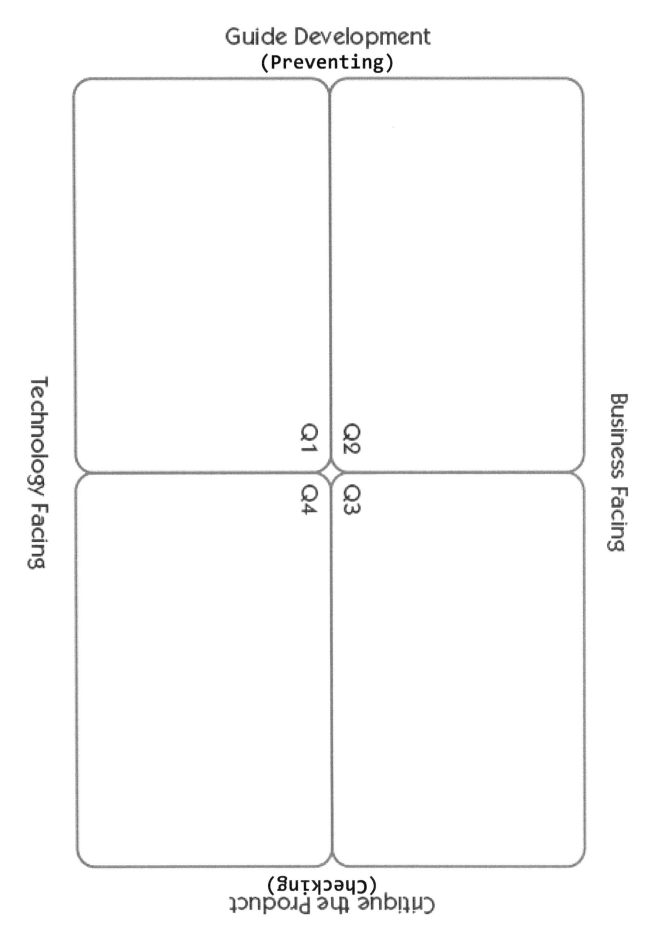

Technology Facing

Business Facing

Q1   Q2

Q4   Q3

Critique the Product
(Checking)

GROUP EXERCISE

Exercise 8: Your 4 Quadrants

Questions

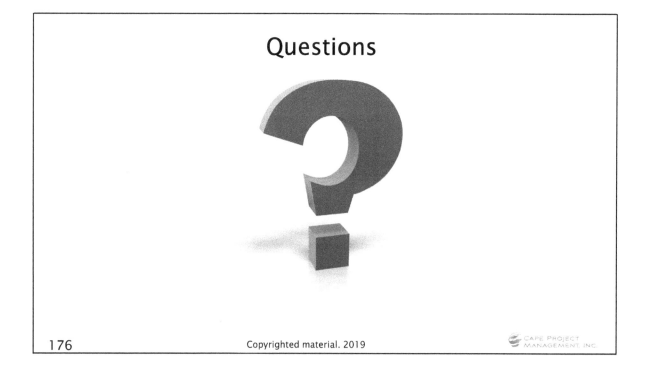

Agile Metrics
Module 7

Agile Principle for Metrics

- In Agile Environment
  - Measure outcomes, not activity.
  - Highest priority is to satisfy the customer through early and continuous delivery of valuable software."
  - Working software is the primary measure of progress.
- In Agile Projects
  - Retrospective at the end of Sprint is more important than metrics
  - Have metrics only for essential aspects
- Benefits of Agile approach to metrics
  - You don't have to spend time documenting all defects or issues
  - Since there is collaboration and less of formal documents, "over the wall" division between the developer and tester is eliminated.
  - Verbally communicated issues are easier to accept than an anonymous incident report.

178

Types Metrics

- Three kinds of Metrics:
  - Informational – tells us what's going on
  - Diagnostic – identifies areas for improvement
  - Motivational – influences behavior
- There are metrics for
  - Customer orientation
  - Business Value
  - Operational Excellence
  - Product Quality
- One metric may function in multiple categories.
  - Example: Delivering high value to customers (informational) can increase team morale (motivational).
- Beware of unintended side-effects.
  - Example: Rewarding people for fixing bugs may result in an increase in bugs, as people create opportunities to earn the rewards.

Most Important Metric: Escaped Defects

- Metric identifying defects that made it into production
- Add to product backlog and prioritize
- Indicates:
  - Inaccurate velocity: team is taking on too much work
  - The team is operating as a "mini-waterfall" project
  - Poor definition of "Done"
- Reduce velocity until the escaping defects metric is reduced

Present Metrics as Information Radiators

☐ Example: Automation Coverage indicating the number of tests that have been automated in that Sprint.

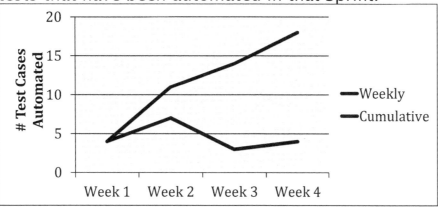

Copyrighted material. 2019
CAPE PROJECT
MANAGEMENT, INC.

Practical tips for Agile Metrics

☐ Define metrics that teams would like to use

☐ Use metrics only for positive results – not to penalize people

☐ Do not compare teams based on metrics

☐ Define metrics that are easy to capture

☐ Select metrics based on maturity level of teams

☐ Metrics should not demoralize team members

☐ Metrics should be transparent

Copyrighted material. 2019

CAPE PROJECT
MANAGEMENT, INC.

DISCUSSION

What metrics does your organization use?
Can you make them more Agile?

Questions

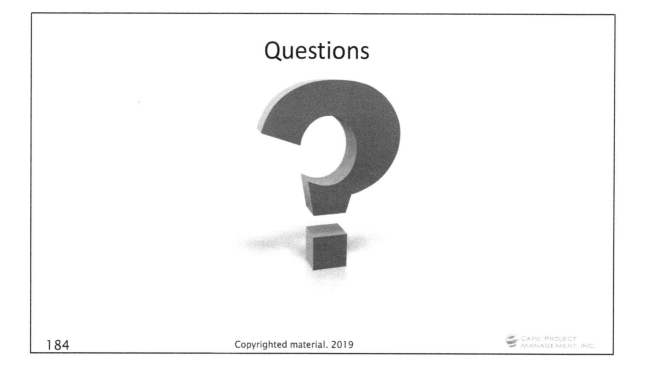

Agile Engineering Implementation
Module 8

Overview

- Identify key practices of highly successful companies
- Plan a quality program by taking the appropriate steps
- Determine the roles and responsibilities of individuals in a quality program
- Agile engineering is all about quality, efficiency and value

Some Basic Quality Program Tenets

- Quality is everyone's business
- It is affected by many but effected by few
- It is important therefore to support the few who are effecting quality
- Educate the many
- Integrate all who are involved

Copyrighted material. 2019

Key Attributes of Quality Planning

- Strategic planning
- Senior management commitment
- Employee roles and responsibilities

Copyrighted material. 2019

Strategic Planning

- Successful companies:
  - Develop detailed plans that they communicate and reinforce throughout the company
  - Have a guided vision
  - Identify a few critical annual objectives and conduct review processes
  - Set goals that support cost reduction and building market share

Senior Management Commitment

- The "key" driver in successful implementation of quality programs
- Top managers (ideally beginning with the CEO) are the leaders of their quality programs and provide vision, support, and recognition
- They must be active in the program, i.e., "walk the talk"

Employee Roles and Responsibilities

- Employees should:
  - Be empowered to make decisions that affect quality
  - Be encouraged to take risks and not fear failure
  - Have a common vision of success
  - Be encouraged to use suggestion systems that act rapidly, provide feedback, and reward implemented suggestions
  - Be trained on a continuous basis

Implications for development teams

- Become generalizing specialists.
  - The implication of whole team testing is that most existing test professionals will need to be prepared to do more than just testing if they want to be involved with Agile projects.
- Be flexible.
  - Agile teams take an iterative and collaborative approach which embraces changing requirements.
- Testers be prepared to work closely with developers.
  - The majority of the testing effort is performed by the Agile delivery team itself, not by independent testers.
- Focus on value-added activities.
  - Agile strategies focus on the value-added activities and minimize if not eliminate the bureaucratic waste which is systemic in many organizations following classical/traditional strategies.

Key Messages

- Value is the primary driver of quality in Agile
- Quality is everyone's business
- Management commitment is key to a successful implementation of quality programs
- Employees need to be empowered to make decisions that affect quality

Copyrighted material. 2019

Forces of Change

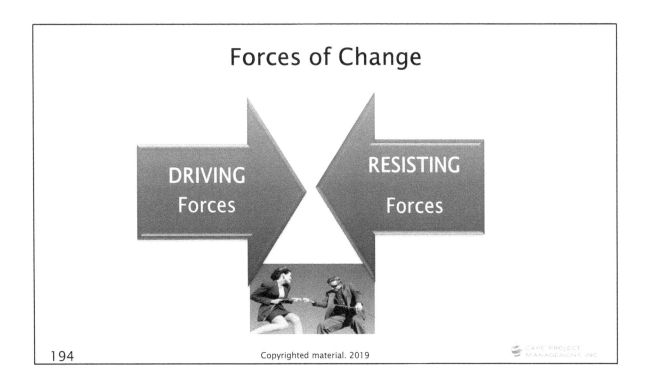

Copyrighted material. 2019

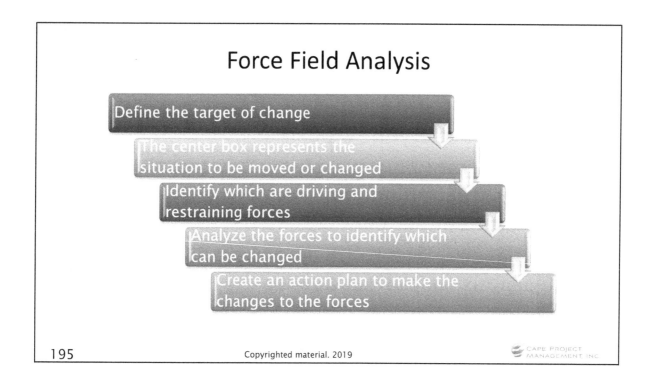

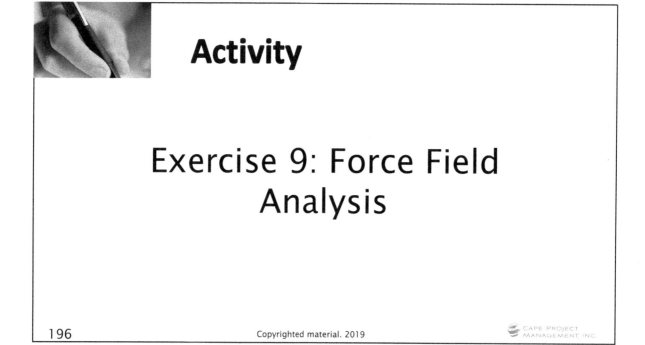

Force Field Analysis

Directions

1. Use the worksheet on the next page.

2. On the center box, the change you are anticipating.

3. List all the forces FOR CHANGE in one column, and all the forces AGAINST CHANGE in another column.

4. Rate the strength of these forces and assign a numerical weight, 1 being the weakest, and 5 being the strongest.

5. When you add the "strength points" of the forces, you'll see the viability of the proposed change.

The tool can be used to help ensure the success of the proposed change by identifying the strength of the forces against the change.

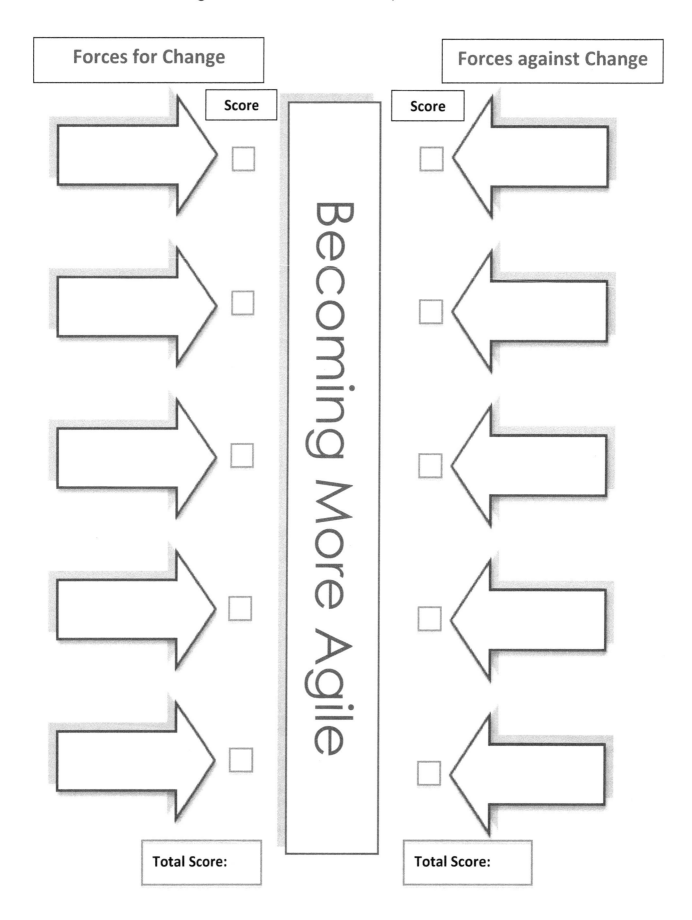

Forces for Change

Forces against Change

Score

Score

Becoming More Agile

Total Score:

Total Score:

GROUP EXERCISE

Copyrighted material. 2019

Preparing for PSD I or CAPe–Dev Exam

- 2/3 of the exam is based upon core Scrum. Take a Scrum training and review the Scrum Guide
  - www.scrumguides.org
- 1/3 is based upon this curriculum.
- Use our Practice Exam 30 days
- You can stop and start as much as you want
- Keep taking it until you get 95%
- PSD 1 exam requires 85% with a single attempt
- CAPE-Dev exam requires 80% and 2 attempts

Login instructions will be delivered via email

Copyrighted material. 2019

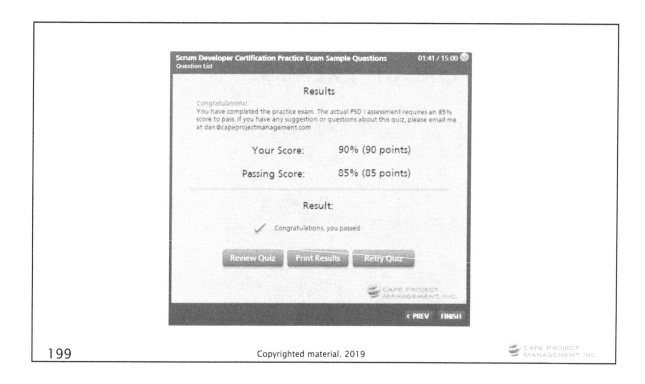

www.ingramcontent.com/pod-product-compliance
Lightning Source LLC
LaVergne TN
LVHW060145070326
832902LV00018B/2964